PROGRAMMING IN NEURAL NETWORKS

PROGRAMMING IN NEURAL NETWORKS

Written by Christopher Bertram,

San Francisco, Ca

Analog Data Enterprises, San Francisco, Ca

PROGRAMMING IN NEURAL NETWORKS

Richard Feynman, Feynman Lectures on Computation, 1970

[Computers] evolves so quickly that even computer scientists cannot keep up with them. It must be confusing for most mathematicians and engineers ... Despite the diversity of applications, methods for attacking difficult problems with computers show a great device, and the name of Computer Sciences will be attached to the discipline as it emerges. However, it must be understood that this is still a field in its structure are still unclear. Students will find many more problems than answers.

TABLE OF CONTENTS

List of Illustrations

Introduction

This project was written in C + + v.11, with Microsoft Visual Studio 2013.

Christopher D. Bertram

Chapter 1

Human brain and Computers

The human brain has the potential to process and store a variety of information. Just like the human brain, the computer can also perform a variety of tasks such as mathematical calculations, complex algorithms and storing essential information (Loe & Wang, 2005). It consists of the right and left brain which enables the body to coordinate and perform various tasks. Likewise, the computer consists of different parts such as the processor, disk drives and the motherboard that help in performing various tasks. According to (Feldman & Feigenbaum 2006), the functions of the brain can be simulated on a digital computer in the equivalent sense in which the behavior of the New York stock market, the weather systems, or the pattern of airline flights over Latin America can.

The human brains consist of neurons which can either be "on" or "off" that help in the transformation of information. Equally, the computer consists of a binary system which transmits signals and enhancing internal communications between different components. In terms of memory capacity, the human brain is also known to grow by stronger synaptic connections and, similarly, the computer memory has the potential to be enlarged by adding computer chips (Feldman & Feigenbaum 2006).

In regard to information storage, the mechanism that is behind information storage is called Long-term potentiating. It involves microscopic chemical adjustments at the synapses that connect neurons to each other. The changes involve the removal of neuro-ceptor units which determine the strength of the signal transmission of any given synapse Richard et al,(2009). The human brain stores information by making adjustments to its neural networks. It grows new dendrites and forms new synapses. Short term memory can be represented by circulating signal feedback loops.

Although technology has revolutionized the world, over reliance of computers hinders the brain from growing. According to Dennett (2008),over reliance on computers, especially for students can lead to long term health issues associated with the brain. This will prevent them from developing into well rounded individuals. When people rely so much on using computers in doing everything, the brain always goes to "sleep". Loe & Wang (2005) argues that, for a human being to have a healthy lifestyle, the brain must be active. However, over relying so much on the computer will hinder the neurons from developing and affect the transmission of information. Furthermore, when the brain is not active, the synaptic connections will not be strong enough to ensure proper functioning of the entire body.

Although over reliance on computers is not appropriate for the brain, we should not entirely shy away from them. Human beings should strike equilibrium between using the computer and making the brain active. Computers should only be used to solve complex issues that require electronic manipulation (Dixit, 2010). Otherwise, the human brain should be actively engaged at all times.

References

Boolos, George S. & Jeffrey, Richard C. (2009). *Computability and Logic*. Cambridge University Press, Cambridge Mass.

Dennett, Daniel C. (2008). *Brainstorms: Philosophical Essays on Mind and Psychology*. MIT Press, Cambridge, Mass.

Dixit,B,J (2010) *Fundamentals of Computers*. Laxmi Publications, Ltd.

Feigenbaum, E.A. and Feldman, J. (2006). *Computers and Thought*. McGraw-Hill Company, New York and San Francisco.

Loe, F. K & Wang, P.Z (2005). Between Mind & Computer: *Fuzzy Science & Engineering*. Sydney: World Scientific.

Chapter 2

Security and Leak Free Neural Networking

Christopher D. Bertram

Abstract

Neural networking has been with us for a long time, in artificial Intelligence (Newell, Shaw, Simon, 1956). The Linked List is used in everything from Word Processing to database design, however: the problems now facing the users are memory leaks and compromises to security. Novel implementation of the Binary Search tree and the latest compiler can solve these issues of security in a science that started as models of the human mind.

1. Although there can never be a true identity condition between mind and brain henceforth the mind body reduction (Searle, 1985), Neural Networks can be constructed to operate as models of nerve cells. Here I present a Binary Search Tree implementation that branch as nerve cells. While any Binary Search Tree is simply a Linked List broken in half; the Binary search tree presented here functions in a different way.

2. There is a multi-axial Binary Search Tree implementation here that has a purpose only to illustrate the point of actual biological cell function. In doing so and breaking with traditional definitions of the Linked List, and Binary search Tree, it has been found to be very useful.

3. The version of Microsoft Visual Studio that implements the latest rules of C++ actually provide the means of leak free programming if the smart pointer system is used for Linked Lists and Binary Search Trees. While it is possible to use older pointers it is the new pointer system that provides the leak free implementation. It is with the leak free pointer implementation here, and the novel Binary Search Tree that provides the security needed in the hostile environment that users of today find themselves entered in to.

4. The base Node of the novel Binary Search Tree presented here is an object called the Neuron. The Neuron here has the input value and the output value as well as a decision value which is Boolean. This could be useful in a variety of ways, such as a second language dictionary, but for the purposes of discussion has only been used for demonstrational purposes only. In so doing the entire demonstration is novel and serves the purpose for illustration for the true neural networking purist.

5. The ultimate encryption use can be operated from the given implementation as discussed in the following. In substitution cypher messaging one word is used for another word and so thusly; in the Neuron of the given implementation one value is an input word and another value is the output word: the substitution word is given in the output of each Neuron in the Binary Search Tree, and so on thusly: operating as an interface between the confidential data and the substitution cypher key, the novel Binary Search Tree acts as the ultimate security software both as a Leak Free system, and the strongest encryption system possible.

6. In an example of how such a security system could be used, a word list of nouns could be substituted for another in a word processor and a secure message could be typed. When printed out, the message would appear in one form that could be unrelated while in actuality the message could contain an entire different meaning when decoded.

7. While the actual example does not contain a cypher substitution system, a method that does so could be constructed. In order to do so one would create an object that reads in the substitution list and places the word list in the Binary Search Tree by using the Set function. The next step would be to create the Print function that would provide the list of words that would be printed for each word on the word list when printed. With the Binary Search Tree loaded a second structure in a word processor would use a Linked List of Objects where a text editor would really be a Linked List of Objects. In the hypothetical cypher substitution system an operator would simply type a message and wouldn't need to be aware of how or what the message would say when printed, nor would the receiver of a message even need to be aware of what the input message contained. There could be a seamless cypher substitution system of messages implemented by simply modifying the example.

Conclusion

A novel implementation of a neural network is presented here that in the Leak Free environment of the latest C++ compilation can be used as the ultimate encryption tool in substitution cypher systems. The novel example is an illustration of how the brain works while learning in branching nervous tissues.

Chapter 3

Experiment: Make a type Neural network as described in Chapter

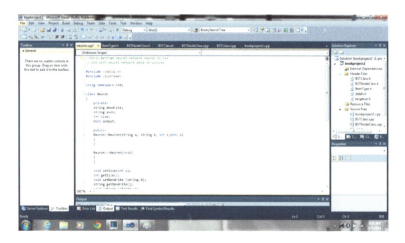

Figure 1. Figure 1 In this photo: The author brings up files after a console project of the files included in the next chapter. The files compile forming a console application and an executable which can run independently.

There should be 8 text files in the project (for each version).

Program.cpp

UserMenu.cpp

Neuron.cpp

TreeFormatter.cpp

UserMenu.h

Neuron.h

TreeFormatter.h

BinarySearchTree.h

This project was written in C++ v.11, with Microsoft Visual Studio 2013.

```cpp
// programm.cpp : Defines the entry point for the console application.
// MSVS 2013

#include "UserMenu.h"
#include <iostream>
#include <cstdlib>
#include <fstream>
#include <string>

void main()
{
    CUserMenu().ProcessUserInput();
}
```

```cpp
// Neuron.h : Header File For Neuron.cpp.
// MSVS 2013


#pragma once

#include <string>
#include <iostream>


class CNeuron
{
public:
        friend std::ostream& operator << (std::ostream& os, const CNeuron& item);
        friend std::ostream& operator << (std::ostream& os, const CNeuron* item);


        CNeuron(
                const std::string& dendrite,
                const std::string& axon,
                const int size,
                const bool output) :
                        m_dendrite(dendrite),
                        m_axon(axon),
                        m_size(size),
                        m_output(output)
        {
        }


        const std::string& GetKey() const { return m_dendrite; };


        const std::string& GetDendrite() const { return m_dendrite; };


        const std::string& GetAxon() const { return m_axon; };


        const bool AxonHillock() const { return m_output; };


        const int GetSize() const { return m_size; };
```

```cpp
private:

        CNeuron& operator = (const CNeuron&) {};


        const std::string m_dendrite;


        const std::string m_axon;


        const bool m_output;


        const int m_size;
};


std::ostream& operator << (std::ostream& os, const CNeuron& item);
std::ostream& operator << (std::ostream& os, const CNeuron* item);
```

```cpp
// Neuron.cpp
// MSVS 2013


#include "Neuron.h"


std::ostream& operator << (std::ostream& os, const CNeuron& item)
{
        return os
                << "[ Dendrit: '" << item.m_dendrite
                << "', Axon: '" << item.m_axon
                << "', Size: " << item.m_size
                << ", AxonHillock: " << (item.m_output ? "yes" : "no")
                << " ]";
}


std::ostream& operator << (std::ostream& os, const CNeuron* item)
{
        return os << *(item);
}
```

```cpp
// UserMenu.cpp
// MSVS 2013

#include "UserMenu.h"

#include "BinarySearchTree.h"
#include "Neuron.h"

#include "TreeFormatter.h"

#include <string>
#include <iostream>

namespace
{

int printMenuHeaderAndAskUser()
{
    int choice = 0;
    std::cout << "\n\n"
        << " ---------------------- \n"
        << " 1. Insertion/Creation \n"
        << " 2. In-Order Traversal \n"
        << " 3. Pre-Order Traversal \n"
        << " 4. Post-Order Traversal \n"
        << " 5. Find and Print \n"
        << " 6. Find and Remove \n"
        << " 7. Exit \n"
        << " ---------------------- \n"
        << " Enter your choice : ";

    std::cin >> choice;

    if (std::cin.fail())
    {
        std::cin.clear();
        std::cin.ignore(std::numeric_limits<std::streamsize>::max(), '\n');
    }
```

```cpp
        return choice;
}


template<typename T>
const T askUserAboutNamedValue(const std::string& key)
{
        T value;
        std::cout << "Enter " << key << " value for node: ";
        std::cin >> value;
        return value;
}


void printNodeValue(const CNeuron* item)
{
        if (item == nullptr)
        {
                std::cout << "Key not found. Try again, please." << std::endl;
        }
        else
        {
                std::cout << "Find result: " << item << std::endl;
        }


}


CUserMenu::CUserMenu(void) :
        m_tree(new CTree())
{
}


CUserMenu::~CUserMenu(void)
{
}


void CUserMenu::ProcessUserInput(void)
{
```

```cpp
std::cout << " -- Valley Process Software Menu -- " << std::endl;


int choice = 0;
while (choice != 7)
{
    int choice = printMenuHeaderAndAskUser();
    switch (choice)
    {
    case 1:
        {
            auto dendrite = askUserAboutNamedValue<std::string>("dendrite");
            auto axon = askUserAboutNamedValue<std::string>("axon");
            auto size = askUserAboutNamedValue<int>("size");
            m_tree->Insert(CNeuron(dendrite, axon, size, true));
        }
        break;
    case 2:
        CTreeFormatter().PrintInOrder(*(m_tree.get()));
        break;
    case 3:
        CTreeFormatter().PrintPreOrder(*(m_tree.get()));
        break;
    case 4:
        CTreeFormatter().PrintPostOrder(*(m_tree.get()));
        break;
    case 5:
        {
            auto key = askUserAboutNamedValue<std::string>("dendrite");
            auto node = m_tree->Find(key);
            printNodeValue(node);
        }
        break;
    case 6:
        {
            auto key = askUserAboutNamedValue<std::string>("dendrite");
            m_tree->Remove(key);
        }
        break;
```

```
            }
        }
    }
```

```cpp
// UserMenu.h
// MSVS 2013


#pragma once

#include <string>
#include <memory>


class CNeuron;
template<typename TItem, typename TKey> class CBinarySearchTree;


class CUserMenu
{
public:
    CUserMenu(void);
    ~CUserMenu(void);


    void ProcessUserInput(void);

private:
    typedef CBinarySearchTree<CNeuron, std::string> CTree;
    const std::unique_ptr<CTree> m_tree;
};
```

```cpp
// BinarySearchTree.h

// MSVS 2013



#pragma once

#include <memory>

template<typename TItem, typename TKey>
class CBinarySearchTree
{
public:
        friend class CTreeFormatter;

        CBinarySearchTree(void) :
                m_root(nullptr),
                m_size(0)
        {};

        ~CBinarySearchTree(void) {};

        int GetSize(void) const { return m_size; }

        bool IsEmpty(void) const { return GetSize() == 0; }

        void Insert(const TItem& item)
        {
                insert(item, m_root);
        }

        void Remove(const TKey& key)
        {
                remove(key, m_root);
        }

        TItem* Find(const TKey& key) const
        {
```

```cpp
        return find(key, m_root);
    }

private:
    class CNode;
    typedef std::unique_ptr<CNode> CNodePtr;
    typedef std::unique_ptr<TItem> TItemPtr;


    class CNode
    {
    public:
        CNode(const TItem& item) :
            m_item(new TItem(item)),
            m_left(nullptr),
            m_right(nullptr)
        {};


        int CompareTo(const TItem& item) const { return CompareTo(item.GetKey()); }


        int CompareTo(const TKey& key) const { return m_item->GetKey().compare(key); }


        TItemPtr m_item;


        CNodePtr m_left;


        CNodePtr m_right;
    };


    void insert(const TItem& item, CNodePtr& node)
    {
        if (!node)
        {
            node.reset(new CNode(item));
            ++m_size;
            return;
        }


        auto compare = node->CompareTo(item);
```

```cpp
        if (compare < 0)
        {
                insert(item, node->m_right);
        }
        else
        {
                insert(item, node->m_left);
        }
    }


TItem* find(const TKey& key, const CNodePtr& node) const
    {
        if (!node)
        {
                return nullptr;
        }

        auto compare = node->CompareTo(key);
        if (compare == 0)
        {
                return node->m_item.get();
        }
        else if (compare < 0)
        {
                return find(key, node->m_right);
        }
        else
        {
                return find(key, node->m_left);
        }
    }


    void remove (const TKey& key, CNodePtr& node)
    {
        if (!node)
        {
                return;
        }
```

```cpp
auto compare = node->CompareTo(key);
if (compare == 0)
{
        if (node->m_left != nullptr && node->m_right != nullptr)
        {
                auto& rightLeft = node->m_right->m_left;
                if (rightLeft.get() == nullptr)
                {
                        rightLeft = std::move(node->m_left);
                        node = std::move(node->m_right);
                }
                else
                {
                        node->m_item = std::move(rightLeft->m_item);
                        remove(node->m_item->GetKey(), rightLeft);
                        return;
                }
        }
        else if (node->m_left != nullptr)
        {
                node = std::move(node->m_left);
        }
        else if (node->m_right != nullptr)
        {
                node = std::move(node->m_right);
        }
        else
        {
                node.release();
        }

        --m_size;
}
else if (compare < 0)
{
        remove(key, node->m_right);
}
```

```cpp
            else
            {
                    remove(key, node->m_left);
            }
    }


    CNodePtr m_root;


    int m_size;
};
```

```cpp
// TreeFormatter.cpp
// MSVS 2013


#include "TreeFormatter.h"


#include <iostream>

void CTreeFormatter::printInOrder(const CTree::CNodePtr& node)
{
        if (node.get() == nullptr)
        {
                return;
        }


        printInOrder(node->m_left);
        std::cout << node->m_item.get() << std::endl;
        printInOrder(node->m_right);
}


void CTreeFormatter::printPreOrder(const CTree::CNodePtr& node)
{
        if (node.get() == nullptr)
        {
                return;
        }


        std::cout << node->m_item.get() << std::endl;
        printPreOrder(node->m_left);
        printPreOrder(node->m_right);
}


void CTreeFormatter::printPostOrder(const CTree::CNodePtr& node)
{
        if (node.get() == nullptr)
        {
                return;
        }
```

```cpp
    printPostOrder(node->m_left);
    printPostOrder(node->m_right);
    std::cout << node->m_item.get() << std::endl;
}
```

```cpp
// TreeFormatter.h
// MSVS 2013


#pragma once

#include "BinarySearchTree.h"
#include "Neuron.h"

#include <string>

class CTreeFormatter
{
public:
    typedef CBinarySearchTree<CNeuron, std::string> CTree;

    void PrintInOrder(const CTree& tree) const { printInOrder(tree.m_root); }
    void PrintPreOrder(const CTree& tree) const { printPreOrder(tree.m_root); }
    void PrintPostOrder(const CTree& tree) const { printPostOrder(tree.m_root); };

private:
    static void printInOrder(const CTree::CNodePtr& node);
    static void printPreOrder(const CTree::CNodePtr& node);
    static void printPostOrder(const CTree::CNodePtr& node);
};
```

```cpp
// programm.cpp : Defines the entry point for the console application.
// MSVS 2010


#include "UserMenu.h"


int main(int argc, char* argv[])
{
    CUserMenu().ProcessUserInput();
    return 0;
}
```

```cpp
// Neuron.cpp MSVS 2010


#include "Neuron.h"


std::ostream& operator << (std::ostream& os, const CNeuron& item)
{
	return os
		<< "[ Dendrit: '" << item.m_dendrite
		<< "', Axon: '" << item.m_axon
		<< "', Size: " << item.m_size
		<< ", AxonHillock: " << (item.m_output ? "yes" : "no")
		<< " ]";
}


std::ostream& operator << (std::ostream& os, const CNeuron* item)
{
	return os << *(item);
}
```

```cpp
// Neuron.h MSVS 2010


#pragma once


#include <string>
#include <iostream>


class CNeuron
{
public:
        friend std::ostream& operator << (std::ostream& os, const CNeuron& item);
        friend std::ostream& operator << (std::ostream& os, const CNeuron* item);


        CNeuron(
                const std::string& dendrite,
                const std::string& axon,
                const int size,
                const bool output) :
                        m_dendrite(dendrite),
                        m_axon(axon),
                        m_size(size),
                        m_output(output)
        {
        }


        const std::string& GetKey() const { return m_dendrite; };


        const std::string& GetDendrite() const { return m_dendrite; };


        const std::string& GetAxon() const { return m_axon; };


        const bool AxonHillock() const { return m_output; };


        const int GetSize() const { return m_size; };


private:
        const std::string m_dendrite;
```

```cpp
        const std::string m_axon;

        const bool m_output;

        const int m_size;
};


std::ostream& operator << (std::ostream& os, const CNeuron& item);
std::ostream& operator << (std::ostream& os, const CNeuron* item);
```

```cpp
// UserMenu.cpp MSVS 2010


#include "UserMenu.h"


#include "BinarySearchTree.h"
#include "Neuron.h"


#include "TreeFormatter.h"


#include <string>
#include <iostream>


namespace
{


int printMenuHeaderAndAskUser()
{
        int choice = 0;
        std::cout << "\n\n"
                << " ---------------------- \n"
                << " 1. Insertion/Creation \n"
                << " 2. In-Order Traversal \n"
                << " 3. Pre-Order Traversal \n"
                << " 4. Post-Order Traversal \n"
                << " 5. Find and Print \n"
                << " 6. Find and Remove \n"
                << " 7. Exit \n"
                << " ---------------------- \n"
                << " Enter your choice : ";


        std::cin >> choice;


        if (std::cin.fail())
        {
                std::cin.clear();
                std::cin.ignore(std::numeric_limits<std::streamsize>::max(), '\n');
        }
```

```cpp
        return choice;
}


template<typename T>
const T askUserAboutNamedValue(const std::string& key)
{
        T value;
        std::cout << "Enter " << key << " value for node: ";
        std::cin >> value;
        return value;
}


void printNodeValue(const CNeuron* item)
{
        if (item == nullptr)
        {
                std::cout << "Key not found. Try again, please." << std::endl;
        }
        else
        {
                std::cout << "Find result: " << item << std::endl;
        }

}


CUserMenu::CUserMenu(void) :
        m_tree(new CTree())
{
}


CUserMenu::~CUserMenu(void)
{
}


void CUserMenu::ProcessUserInput(void)
{
        std::cout << " -- Valley Process Software Menu -- " << std::endl;
```

```cpp
while(true)
{
        int choice = printMenuHeaderAndAskUser();

        switch (choice)
        {
        case 1:
                {
                        auto dendrite = askUserAboutNamedValue<std::string>("dendrite");

                        auto axon = askUserAboutNamedValue<std::string>("axon");

                        auto size = askUserAboutNamedValue<int>("size");

                        m_tree->Insert(CNeuron(dendrite, axon, size, true));
                }
                break;
        case 2:
                CTreeFormatter().PrintInOrder(*(m_tree.get()));

                break;
        case 3:
                CTreeFormatter().PrintPreOrder(*(m_tree.get()));

                break;
        case 4:
                CTreeFormatter().PrintPostOrder(*(m_tree.get()));

                break;
        case 5:
                {
                        auto key = askUserAboutNamedValue<std::string>("dendrite");

                        auto node = m_tree->Find(key);

                        printNodeValue(node);
                }
                break;
        case 6:
                {
                        auto key = askUserAboutNamedValue<std::string>("dendrite");

                        m_tree->Remove(key);
                }
                break;
        case 7:
                return;
```

```
            default:
                break;
        }
    }
}
```

```cpp
// UserMenu.h MSVS 2010


#pragma once


#include <string>
#include <memory>


class CNeuron;
template<typename TItem, typename TKey> class CBinarySearchTree;


class CUserMenu
{
public:
        CUserMenu(void);
        ~CUserMenu(void);


        void ProcessUserInput(void);

private:
        typedef CBinarySearchTree<CNeuron, std::string> CTree;
        const std::unique_ptr<CTree> m_tree;
};
```

```cpp
// BinarySearchTree.h MSVS

#pragma once

#include <memory>

class CTreeFormatter;

template<typename TItem, typename TKey>
class CBinarySearchTree
{
public:
        friend class CTreeFormatter;

        CBinarySearchTree(void) :
                m_root(nullptr),
                m_size(0)
        {};

        ~CBinarySearchTree(void) {};

        int GetSize(void) const { return m_size; }

        bool IsEmpty(void) const { return GetSize() == 0; }

        void Insert(const TItem& item)
        {
                insert(item, m_root);
        }

        void Remove(const TKey& key)
        {
                remove(key, m_root);
        }

        TItem* Find(const TKey& key) const
        {
                return find(key, m_root);
```

```cpp
        }

private:

        class CNode;

#if _MSC_VER == 1600
        struct CNodeDeleter
        {
                void operator()(CNode* ptr) { delete ptr; }
        };


        typedef std::unique_ptr<CNode, CNodeDeleter> CNodePtr;
#else
        typedef std::unique_ptr<CNode> CNodePtr;
#endif


        typedef std::unique_ptr<TItem> TItemPtr;


        class CNode
        {
        public:
                CNode(const TItem& item) :
                        m_item(new TItem(item)),
                        m_left(nullptr),
                        m_right(nullptr)
                {
                };


                int CompareTo(const TItem& item) const { return CompareTo(item.GetKey()); }


                int CompareTo(const TKey& key) const { return m_item->GetKey().compare(key); }


                TItemPtr m_item;


                CNodePtr m_left;


                CNodePtr m_right;
        };
```

```cpp
void insert(const TItem& item, CNodePtr& node)
{
        if (node.get() == nullptr)
        {
                node.reset(new CNode(item));
                ++m_size;
                return;
        }


        auto compare = node->CompareTo(item);
        if (compare < 0)
        {
                insert(item, node->m_right);
        }
        else
        {
                insert(item, node->m_left);
        }
}


TItem* find(const TKey& key, const CNodePtr& node) const
{
        if (node.get() == nullptr)
        {
                return nullptr;
        }


        auto compare = node->CompareTo(key);
        if (compare == 0)
        {
                return node->m_item.get();
        }
        else if (compare < 0)
        {
                return find(key, node->m_right);
        }
        else
```

```cpp
        {
            return find(key, node->m_left);
        }
    }


    void remove (const TKey& key, CNodePtr& node)
    {
        if (node.get() == nullptr)
        {
            return;
        }


        auto compare = node->CompareTo(key);
        if (compare == 0)
        {
            if (node->m_left != nullptr && node->m_right != nullptr)
            {
                if (node->m_right->m_left.get() == nullptr)
                {
                    node->m_right->m_left = std::move(node->m_left);
                    node = std::move(node->m_right);
                }
                else
                {
                    node->m_item = std::move(node->m_right->m_left->m_item);
                    remove(node->m_item->GetKey(), node->m_right->m_left);
                    return;
                }
            }
            else if (node->m_left != nullptr)
            {
                node = std::move(node->m_left);
            }
            else if (node->m_right != nullptr)
            {
                node = std::move(node->m_right);
            }
            else
```

```
                        {
                                node.release();
                        }


                        --m_size;
                }
                else if (compare < 0)
                {
                        remove(key, node->m_right);
                }
                else
                {
                        remove(key, node->m_left);
                }
        }


        CNodePtr m_root;


        int m_size;
};
```

```cpp
// TreeFormatter.cpp MSVS 2010


#include "TreeFormatter.h"

#include <iostream>

void CTreeFormatter::printInOrder(const CTree::CNodePtr& node)
{
        if (node.get() == nullptr)
        {
                return;
        }


        printInOrder(node->m_left);
        std::cout << node->m_item.get() << std::endl;
        printInOrder(node->m_right);
}


void CTreeFormatter::printPreOrder(const CTree::CNodePtr& node)
{
        if (node.get() == nullptr)
        {
                return;
        }


        std::cout << node->m_item.get() << std::endl;
        printPreOrder(node->m_left);
        printPreOrder(node->m_right);
}


void CTreeFormatter::printPostOrder(const CTree::CNodePtr& node)
{
        if (node.get() == nullptr)
        {
                return;
        }
```

```cpp
    printPostOrder(node->m_left);

    printPostOrder(node->m_right);

    std::cout << node->m_item.get() << std::endl;

}
```

```cpp
// TreeFormatter.h MSVS 2010

#pragma once

#include "BinarySearchTree.h"
#include "Neuron.h"

#include <string>

class CTreeFormatter
{
public:
	typedef CBinarySearchTree<CNeuron, std::string> CTree;

	void PrintInOrder(const CTree& tree) const { printInOrder(tree.m_root); }
	void PrintPreOrder(const CTree& tree) const { printPreOrder(tree.m_root); }
	void PrintPostOrder(const CTree& tree) const { printPostOrder(tree.m_root); };

private:
	static void printInOrder(const CTree::CNodePtr& node);
	static void printPreOrder(const CTree::CNodePtr& node);
	static void printPostOrder(const CTree::CNodePtr& node);
};
```

Appendix

Curriculum Vitae

UNIVERSITY OF CALIFORNIA, BERKELEY, Berkeley, California

Clinical Laboratory Scientist Preparatory Program *(Currently pursuing certificate in Clinical Laboratory Scientist Preparatory Program)*

SAN FRANCISCO STATE UNIVERSITY, San Francisco, California

Bachelor of Science in General Biology w/ Minor Computer Science

HEALD INSTITUTE OF TECHNOLOGY, San Francisco, California

Associate in Applied Science, Electronics & Networking Technology *(Dual Major)*

MERRITT COLLEGE, Oakland, California

Associate in Science, Math/ Natural Science & Associate in Art, Social and Behavioral Sciences *(Dual Major)*

AMERICAN RIVER COLLEGE, Carmichael, California

Associate in Science, General Science

www.ingramcontent.com/pod-product-compliance
Lightning Source LLC
Chambersburg PA
CBHW050937060326
40689CB00040B/628